Acceptance

A Spiritual
Way of Life

Christine A. Adams

Copyright

To request permission, contact the publisher at

hanleyadamspublishing@gmail.com

Paperback ISBN: 979-8-9855267-8-3

Ebook ISBN: 979-8-9855267-9-0

First paperback edition March 2023

Edited by MD Hanley

Word Cloud Art Designed by MD Hanley

Cover photography by Harrison Hanley

https://www.harrywander.com/

Graphics by https://www.wordclouds.com/

Hanley-Adams Publishing

Boxboro, MA 01719

www.hanleyadamspublishing.com

Foreword

Acceptance: A Spiritual Way of Life is a companion book to my first book in the series, Gratitude: A Spiritual Way of Life. Why? Acceptance and Gratitude are intrinsically connected. They walk side by side! When you can find gratitude for each moment of your life, you find acceptance for the changes that are happening. Non- acceptance causes pain and distances us from a loving God. It is a spiritual issue!

But what about accepting those difficult times - the unexpected losses, missed opportunities, irreversible tragedies, the death of a loved one, the attitude, behavior or unwise choices of us, or others, or our own mortality. We can turn our life and our will over to God – finding gratitude in the moment.

When we can accept life as it unfolds with emphasis on what God is doing for us rather than on what we do not have, we can find peace and joy. Our task is to have the wisdom to discern what can't be changed and what can. When blocked by our own human desires, we can ask God for guidance. Look to all things in nature, with the seasons – all things change in a miraculous cycle.

We accept in faith and humility that there are some things that only God can understand. God is Love Itself. A beneficent benefactor and You are His child and live in His Love.

Acceptance involves the relinquishment of Self, the Ego. We willingly turn our will and our life over to a power greater than ourselves - accepting we are <u>not</u> God. However, we can always fight for the greater good by spreading Love through positive change. These acts of Love add spiritual purpose to our life.

Humility is also a necessary part of spiritual living. Acceptance includes the critical knowledge that, as humans, we are not infallible, all knowing and perfect. We will make mistakes. Forgive yourself and forgive others. Then go on!

Sometimes we can't see around the corners of our life. But we can welcome, accept and honor the changes. Trust in your future and have hope. Accept yourself and others. Learn from your anger. Know that God's Love prevails through every moment of your existence. Even this moment that you and I share right now. God blesses us now!

1.

When we accept life on life's terms, we find gratitude! Acceptance leads to gratitude and gratitude leads to acceptance. Thankful people live each moment in a positive, hopeful light with a sense of wonder.

2.

Here is the secret! Count your blessings and watch them grow! Gratitude brings you a sense of peace, a quietness of the soul. It attracts more blessings. An acceptance of what is good.

3.

Accepting your life as it unfolds, with emphasis on what God is doing for you rather than emphasis on what you do not have, leads to happiness.

4.

But how do we accept the most difficult situations in our lives you ask? We accept with faith and humility - by giving all our disappointments, failures, sorrows, and worries over to God.

failures

How to accept

worries

giving all worries

disappointments

over to God

giving all disappointments

failures

worries

most difficult situations

faith

worries

humility

worries

We accept with humility

We accept with faith

We accept with faith

most difficult situations

giving all sorrows

giving all disappointments

over to God

faith

giving all worries

giving all failures

We accept with faith

situations

you ask?

giving all worries

We accept with humility

Accepting

giving all

you ask?

faith

in our lives

We accept with faith

giving all failures

in our lives

How to accept

We accept

over to God

over to God

disappointments

worries

humility

disappointments

you ask?

giving all sorrows

humility

5.

Acceptance is a spiritual way of life, a constant prayer, as we turn our life and our will over to God - finding gratitude in the moment.

6.

If we believe in God as a power greater than ourselves, we can humbly ask for guidance in all decisions. Always knowing, believing that the God who took care of us yesterday will be there today and tomorrow.

7.

First, we have to accept what we can't change. We <u>can't</u> change missed opportunities, irreversible tragedies, the death of a loved one, the attitude, behavior or unwise choices of others, and, of course, old age and death.

8.

Secondly, our task is to change the things we <u>can</u>. We can change ourselves, our behavior, habits and thinking. And at times we can change our circumstances if we have courage and determination.

9.

There are those times that we do not have the power to change a situation and our only choice is to accept. So, at that time, we need the wisdom to determine what can be changed and what can't. Sometimes, we can be blinded by our human desires and need guidance to see clearly. Ask God for help!

10.

Nature teaches us that we need to accept change! Like the seasons, our life goes from the cold months of Winter, to the warmth of Spring and Summer, to the fullness of Fall and back to the bleak cold again.

11.

In time, things can go from birth to death, youth to old age, hate to love, misunderstanding to understanding, rebellion to resolve, and despair to happiness. Accept change, it only hurts when we resist it.

12.

The only permanence In life seems to be its flux of imperma- nence. Our life will be full of sur- prises, mystery, as it shifts and changes. How we flow with it suggests that "acceptance" is our primary spiritual challenge.

13.

You might ask, "What is God's will for me? What does God want me to do with my life? To teach, to build, to lead others? Perhaps, but as we teach, build or lead society, we need to accept our life as it unfolds.

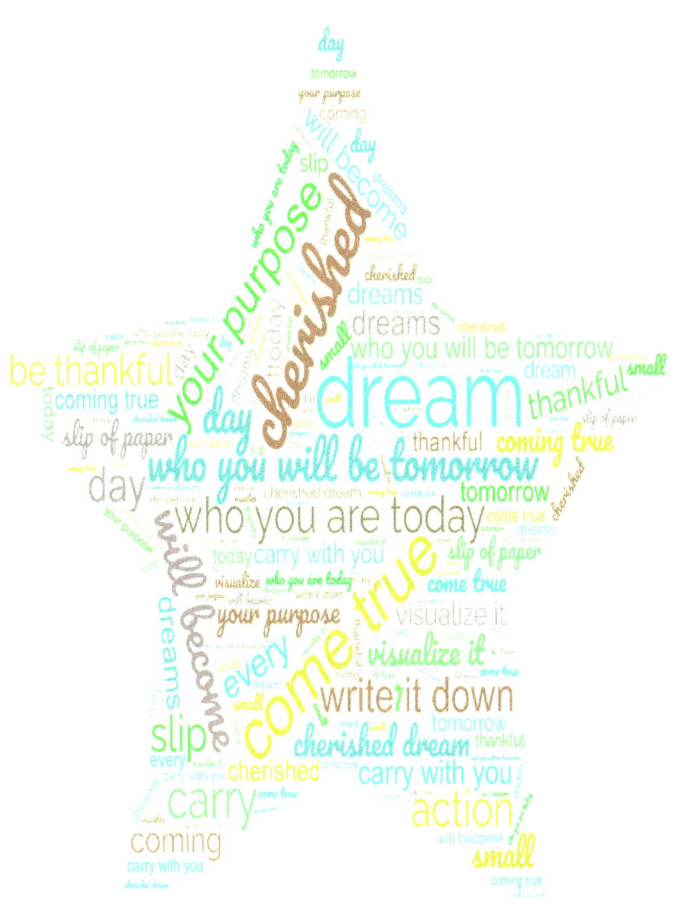

14.

But what about those unexplainable, illogical, happenings, or the unwanted losses that come to all of us? We accept in faith and humility that there are some things that only God can understand. We are not God!

15.

God Is Love, Itself. A beneficent benefactor and You are His Child and live in his love.

16.

Faith in a power greater than ourselves - the creator of this magnificent universe, involves the relinquishment of Self, the Ego. By turning our will and our life over to our father, God, through Jesus Christ, we establish that we are <u>not</u> God.

17.

Does that mean that we accept everything and stop fighting for change? No! It is noble to fight for positive change. We can fight for the better good! If God is Love and we are living in love, spreading love, we add spiritual purpose to our lives.

18.

Non-acceptance happens when we can't accept a change that can't be reversed. Like the death of a loved one, sudden loss of health, sometimes loss of relationships, or changed social standing, or the struggle with our own mortality.

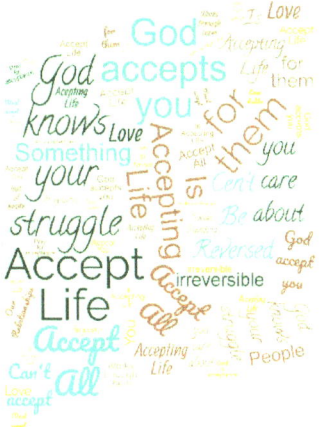

19.

There are times you might feel like a victim because so many bad things are happening. You might feel mad at God thinking you are being punished. At this time, your faith is being tested. Hold on!

20.

Remember God is not doing bad things to you. You are God's child! God's will for you is joy! God is Love!

21.

Humility is a necessary part of spiritual living - acceptance includes the critical knowledge that as humans we are not infallible, all knowing and perfect. We are simply human. Let us stop trying to be perfect.

22.

Just as we accept our humanity when we make mistakes, we need to also accept our spirituality. Know that we are children of God. And, because we are, accept that God, the Father's will for us is joy.

23.

Honest self-reflection helps us achieve acceptance. Prayer and meditation bring us back to God. Check your thoughts. Are you living in the past? Are you incessantly blaming yourself for not being perfect?

24.

Slow down! Retreat from the world's noise and your worries. Seek a place of peace - silence. The only reality is this moment! God is in the silence of this moment. Go there now!

25.

Each day is alive with possibilities. Each moment is an extraordinary gift. You are right where you are supposed to be right now. This moment is all you have. Cherish it!

26.

When you need to change something In your life, don't be discouraged. Pray for guidance. In nature, there is always a new beginning, a flower goes from a seed, to a beautiful blossom. In time, that blossom fades and dies leaving new seeds to continue the beauty.

27.

Sometimes we can't see around the corners of our life. Be patient. Welcome, accept, and honor the changes. Change only hurts when we resist it. Think of all that you have been, who you are now, and what you will be.

28.

You are the only person in charge of your life. Love yourself! Be productive and positive. A small miracle will happen when you live with acceptance and gratitude. You will be "accepted" by others. When you love yourself, you attract love and acceptance!

29.

It's time to trust In your own future. In the past you came through some difficulties, some changes that seemed hopeless, but these difficult times turned out to bring you blessings. Have hope!

30.

As you accept yourself, extend that acceptance to others. Give your loved ones the freedom to grow, to make changes In their life. When you hold them too tight, you inhibit their growth.

31.

Unsolicited advice can be taken as criticism. Try not to force your good intentions on others. Let them discover their own path.

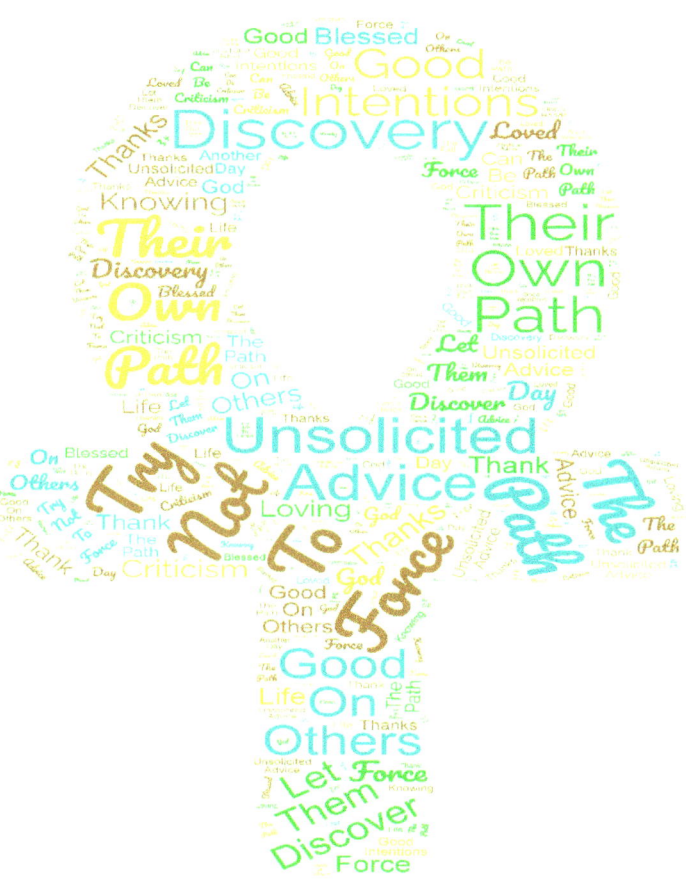

32.

Observe you're anger! Examine the circumstances that Initiated that anger. Usually we are hurt when we are angry. What does anger teach you about yourself?

33.

Forgive yourself, and others for human mistakes. Understand that forgiveness has already taken place in the mind and heart of God. It's only a matter of time until we catch up - whether it is in this world or in the next. Forgiveness is a gift to you!

34.

Contentment is not seeking all you want, but enjoying what you already have. Untangle you're anxiety, release your tension. Rest and play whenever you can.

35.

When suffering and tragedy
come to you, ask God for help to
endure the pain. Trust that
good can emerge from tragedy
and new life from the dying.
Trust in the future.

Trust in Good Ask Trust in God Good Emerges Trust in the Future
Trust in the Future Good Suffering and Change Tragedy
Suffering Change the world! Ask God for Help
Ask Goodness Prevails Appreciation Share the gift Ask Help
Kindness The Future Trust appreciate Good Emerges Change Good Emerges
You Life Emerges Goodness Help to Endure
Acceptance Goodness

36.

When like the night, you are surrounded by darkness and life seems hopeless, trust that at dawn a bright new day will come. In Spring the flowers will bloom. God's Love prevails through every moment of our existence.

37.

Let us give thanks for this moment! For your sight to see, your ability to read and understand my words. For my sight to see and write these words. Together, we have quietly accepted a peaceful moment of God's love.

— *Notes* —

Notes

— Notes —

Notes

— Notes —

Also by Christine A. Adams

Gratitude Therapy: A Spiritual Way of Life

Seasons: Spiritual Meditations For

Winter, Spring, Summer, and Fall

Spirituality: A Life Force

ABC's of Grief – A Handbook for Survivors

Let Go and Let God

Teacher of God

Holy Relationships

Living in Love

September Love

Claiming Your Own Life

School Factory

Love, Infidelity, and Sexual Addiction

Gratitude Therapy

One Day At A Time

Learning To Be A Good Friend

Happy To Be Me

Worry, Worry, Go Away

God Made Us One By One

Watch for more at her website!

http://www.christineaadams.com/

About the Author

Christine A. Adams, M.A., has been writing about issues of addiction, relationships, spirituality, and education for over 32 years. She has over 2,000,000 separate books and pamphlets in print with works published in 52 countries translated into 35 languages. Chris, an English teacher, was also formerly trained as an addiction counselor in 1986. However, most of her writing parallels her life experiences. Her early writings were about the alcoholic marriage, adult children of alcoholics, teen alcoholism, and sexual addiction. Then came books about spirituality, relationships, grief therapy and education.

In addition, she has produced 4 very popular Elf Help children's books: Happy To Be Me, Learning To Be A Good Friend, Worry, Worry, Go Away, and God Made

Us One By One. One of her best-known recovery books is the adult Elf Help gift book, One Day At A Time Therapy which is still selling in places like Taiwan, China, Portugal, the Netherlands, Austria, Sweden, Indonesia, and Brazil.

Her other books include: Gratitude: A Spiritual Way of Life, Spirituality: A Life Force, Seasons: Spiritual Meditations for Winter, Spring, Summer, and Fall, Let Go, Let God, Teacher of God, Holy Relationships, and ABC's of Grief: A Handbook For Survivors. Other books include a fictional narrative, based on her years of teaching, called The School Factory, and romantic novel, September Love. Visit her at www.christineaadams.com or go to www.hanleyadamspublishing.com to find all her books.

Dedication

Robert J. Butch

(1942 - 2021

To Robert J Butch, my late husband, who made "a way of life" living the concepts of this Acceptance book. Through sobriety and daily meditations, he always believed "Life is Good." Through two years of a debilitating terminal illness, he remained appreciative of life and love and actually lived with gratitude and acceptance each day-"One Day At A Time". Today, I am thankful to have been beside him for nearly thirty years. Our loving memories inspire me and still sustain me today!

John F. McKenna

(1939 – 2023)

To John F. McKenna, the McKenna family patriarch, whose diligence, generosity, and humility are legend. My brother, my friend, who over the years has gained the respect of family, business associates, and friends. He was a constant pillar of strength, much like the stone walls he built in York, Maine. For his strength, wisdom and love, I am forever grateful.